More Fruits of Solitude

MORE
Fruits of Solitude:
BEING
The Second PART
OF
REFLECTIONS
AND
MAXIMS,
Relating to the
CONDUCT
OF
Human Life.

LONDON:
Printed and Sold, by the *Assigns* of
J. Sowle, at the *Bible* in *George-Yard, Lombard-Street,* 1718.

THE INTRODUCTION TO THE READER.

THE Title of this Treatise shows, there was a former of the same Nature; and the Author hopes, he runs no Hazzard in Recommending Both to his Reader's Perusal. He is well aware

The Introduction.

of the low Reckoning, the Labours of Indifferent Authors are under, at a Time, when hardly any Thing passes for Currant, that is not Calculated to Flatter the Sharpness of Contending Parties. He is also sensible, that Books grow a very Drug, where they cannot Raise and Support their Credit, by their own Usefulness; and how far this will be able to do it, he knows not; yet he thinks himself

The Introduction.

self tollerably safe in making it Publick, in three Respects.

Firſt, *That the Purchaſe is ſmall, and the Time but little, that is requiſite to read It.*

Next, *Though ſome Men ſhould not find it reliſh'd* High Enough *for their finer Wits, or warmer Pallats, it may not perhaps be* Uſeleſs *to thoſe of lower Flights, and who are* Leſs *Engaged in publick Heats.*

The Introduction.

Lastly, The Author honestly aims at as General a Benefit, as the Thing will bear; to Youth *espeially, whether he hits the Mark or not: And that without the least Ostentation, or any private Regards.*

Let not Envy mis-interpret his Intention, and he will be accountable for all other Faults.

Vale.

More

More Fruits of Solitude:
BEING
The Second PART.
OF
REFLETIONS
AND
MAXIMS.

The Right Moralist.

1. A Right Moralist, is a Great and Good Man, but for that reason he is *rarely* to be found.

2. There

2. There are a sort of People, that are *fond* of the Character, who, in my Opinion, have but little Title to it.

3. They think it enough, not to *defraud* a Man of his Pay, or *betray* his Friend; but never consider, That the Law forbids the one at his Peril, and that Vertue is *seldom* the reason of the other.

4. But certainly he that *Covets*, can no more be a Moral Man, than he that *Steals*; since he does so in his Mind. Nor can he be one that Robs his Neighbour of his *Credit*, or that craf-

Reflections and Maxims 3
craftily undermines him of his *Trade* or *Office*.

5. If a Man pays his Taylor, but Debuaches his Wife; Is he a currant Moralist?

6. But what shall we say of the Man that *Rebels* against his Father, is an *Ill Husband*, or an *Abusive Neighbour*; one that's *Lavish* of his Time, of his Health, and of his Estate, in which his Family is so nearly concerned? Must he go for a Right Moralist, because he pays his Rent well?

7. I would ask some of those Men of Morals, Whe-

ther he that Robs *God* and *Himself* too, though he should not defraud his Neighbour, be the Moral Man?

8. Do I owe my self Nothing? And do I not owe All to God? And if paying what we owe, makes the Moral Man, Is it not fit we should begin to render our Dues, *where* we owe our very Beginning; ay, our *All*?

9. The *Compleat* Moralist begins with *God*; he gives him his Due, his *Heart*, his *Love* his *Service*; the Bountiful Giver of his *Well-Being*, as well as

Reflections and Maxims. 5

10. He that lives without a Sense of this Dependency and Obligation, cannot be a Moral Man, because he does not make his Returns, of Love and Obedience: as becomes an honest and a sensible Creature: Which very Term Implies he is not his own; and it cannot be very honest to mis-imploy another's Goods.

11. But can there be no Debt, but to a fellow Creature? Or, will our Exactness in paying those *Dribling* ones, while we neglect our weightier Obligations, Cancel the Bonds we lye

12. As *Judgments* are paid before *Bonds*, and *Bonds* before *Bills* or *Book-Debts*, so the Moralist considers his Obligations according to their several *Dignities*.

In the first place, *Him* to whom he owes himself. Next, *himself*, in his Health and Livelihood. Lastly, His other Obligations, whether *Relational* or *Pecuniary*; doing to others, to the Extent of his Ability, as he would have them do unto him.

13. In short, The *Moral Man* is he that *Loves God*

above All, and *his Neighbour as himself*, which fulfils both Tables at once.

The World's able Man.

14. It is by some thought, the Character of an Able Man, to be *Dark, and not Understood*. But I am sure that is not fair Play.

15. If he be so by *Silence*, 'tis better; but if by *Disguises*, 'tis *insincere* and *hateful*.

16. Secrecy is one thing, *false Lights* is another.

17. The honest Man, that is rather free, than open, is ever

ever to be preferr'd, especially when *Sense* is at Helm.

18. The Glorying of the other Humour is in a *Vice* For it is not Humane to be *Cold, Dark* and *Unconversable.* I was a going to say, they are like *Pick-Pockets* in a Crowd, where a Man must ever have his *Hand* on his Purse; or as *Spies* in a Garrison, that if not prevented betrays it.

19. They are the *Reverse* of Human Nature, and yet this is the present World's *Wise Man* and Politician: Excellent Qualities for *Lapland,* where, they say, Witches,
tho'

Reflections and Maxims. 9
tho' not many Cunjurors, dwell.

20. Like *Highway-Men*, that rarely Rob without *Vizards*, or in the *same* Wigs and Cloaths, but have a *Dress* for every Enterprize.

21. At best, he may be a *Cunning* Man, which is a sort of *Lurcher* in the Politicks.

22. He is never too hard for the *Wise* Man upon the *Square*, for that is out of his Element, and puts him quite by his Skill. Nor are *Wise* Men ever catch'd by him, but when they trust him.

23. But

23. But as *Cold* and *Close* as he seems, he can and will please all, if he gets by it, tho' it should neither please God nor himself at bottom.

24. He is for every Cause that brings him Gain, but Implacable if disappointed of Success.

25. And what he cannot hinder, he will be sure to Spoil, by over-doing it.

26. None so *Zealous* then as he, for that which he cannot abide.

27. What

Reflections and Maxims. 11

27. What is it he will not, or cannot do, to hide his true Sentiments.

28. For his Interest, he refuses no Side or Party; and will take the *Wrong* by the Hand, when t'other wont do, with as *good* a *Grace* as the Right.

29. Nay, he commonly chuses the *Worst*, because that brings the best Bribe: His Cause being ever Money.

30. He Sails with all *Winds*, and is never out of his way, where any thing is to be had.

31. A

31. A *Privateer* indeed, and every-where a very Bird of *Prey*.

32. True to nothing but *himself*, and false to all Persons and Parties, to serve his own Turn.

33. Talk with him as often as you please, he will never pay you in good Coin; for 'tis either *False* or *Clipt*.

34. But to give a *False* Reason for any thing, let my Reader never learn of him, no more than to give a Brass half Crown for a good one: Not only because it is not true, but because it *Deceives* the Person to whom it is given;

Reflections and Maxims. 13
given; which I take to be an *Immorality*.

35. *Silence* is much more preferable, for it *saves* the Secret, as well as the Person's Honour.

36. Such as give themselves the Latitude of saying what they do not mean, come to be *errant Jockeys* at more things than one; but in *Religion* and *Politicks*, 'tis most pernicious.

37. To hear two Men talk the *Reverse* of their own Sentiments, with all the good Breeding and Appearance of Friendship imagiable,

ginable, on purpose to *Cozen* or *Pump* each other, is to a Man of *Virtue* and *Honour*, one of the Melancholiest, as well as most Nauseous, Thing in the World.

38. But that it should be the Character of an Able Man, is to *Disinherit Wisdom*, and Paint out our Degeneracy to the Life, by setting up Fraud, an errant *Imposter*, in her room.

39. The Tryal of Skill between these two is, who shall believe *least* of what t'other says; and he that has the *Weakness*, or good Nature, to *give* out *first*, (*viz.* to *believe* any thing t'other

Reflections and Maxims. 15
t'other fays) is look'd upon to be *Trick'd*.

40. I cannot fee the *Policy*, any more than the Neceffity, of a Man's Mind always giving the Lye to his Mouth, or his Mouth ever giving the falfe Allarms of his Mind: For no Man can be long believed, that teaches all Men to diftruft him; and fince the Ableft have fometimes need of Credit, where lies the Advantage of their Politick *Cant* or *Banter* upon Mankind?

41. I remember a Paffage of one of Queen *Elizabeth*'s Great Men, as Advice to his

his Friend; *The Advantage,* says he, *I had upon others at Court, was, that I always spoke as* I thought, *which being not* believed *by them, I both preserv'd a* good Conscience, *and suffered* no Damage *from that Freedom:* which, as it shows the Vice to be Older than our Times, so that Gallant Man's Integrity, to be the best way of avoiding it.

42. To be sure it is wise, as well as Honest, neither to flatter other Men's Sentiments, nor *Dissemble* and less *Contradict* our own.

43. To hold ones Tongue, or speak Truth, or talk only

only of indifferent Things, is the *Fairest* Conversation.

44. *Women* that rarely go abroad without *Vizard-Masks*, have none of the best Reputation. But when we consider what all this *Art* and *Disguise* are for, it epually hightens the *Wise* Man's *Wonder* and Aversion: Perhaps it is to *betray* a Father, a Brother, a Master, a Friend, a Neighbour, or ones own Party.

45. A fine Conquest! what Noble *Grecians* and *Romans* abhorr'd: As if Government could not *subsist* without Knavery, and that Knaves

Knaves were the *Usefullest* Props to it; tho' the basest, as well as greatest, Perversion of the *Ends* of it.

46. But that it should become a *Maxim*, shows but too grosly the Corruption of the Times.

47. I confess I have heard the stile of a *Useful Knave*, but ever took it to be a silly or a knavish Saying; at least an *Excuse* for Knavery.

48. It is as reasonable to think a *Whore* makes the *best Wife*, as a *Knave* the best *Officer*.

49. Be-

49. Besides, Employing Knaves, *Encourages* Knavery instead of Punishing it; and *Alienates* the Reward of Vertue. Or, at least, must make the World believe, the Country yields not honest Men enough, able to serve her.

50. Art thou a Magistrate? Prefer such as have *clean* Characters where they live, and of Estates to *secure* a just Discharge of their Trusts; that are under no Temptation to *strain* Points, for a Fortune: For sometimes such may be found, *sooner* than they are Employed.

51. Art

51. Art thou a Private Man? Contract thy Acquaintance in a narrow Compass, and chuse Those for the Subjects of it, that are Men of Principles; such as will make full Stops, where Honour will not lead them on; and that had rather bear the Disgrace of not being *thorow Paced* Men, than *forfeit* their Peace and Reputation by a *base* Compliance.

The Wise Man.

52. The *Wise* Man Governs himself by the *Reason* of his Case, and because what he does is *Best*: Best, in a
Moral

Moral and Prudent, not a *Sinister* Sense.

53. He proposes just Ends, and employs the *fairest* and *probablest* Means and Methods to attain them.

54. Tho' you cannot always penetrate his Design, or his Reasons for it, yet you shall ever see his Actions of a *Piece*, and his Performances like a *Workman*. They will bear the *Touch* of Wisdom and Honour, as often as they are tryed.

55. He scorns to serve himself by *Indirect Means*, or be an *Interloper* in Government,

vernment, since Just Enterprises never want any Just *Ways* to succeed them.

56. To do Evil, that Good may come of it, *is* for *Bunglers* in Politicks, as well as Morals.

57. Like those Surgeons, that will cut off an Arm they can't Cure, to *hide* their Ignorance and save their Credit.

58. The *Wise* Man is *Cautious*, but not Cunning; *Judicious*, but not Crafty; making Vertue the *Measure* of using his Excellent Understanding in the Conduct of his Life.

59. The

59. The *Wise* Man is equal, ready, but not *officious*; has in every Thing an Eye to *Sure Footing*. He offends *no Body*, nor *easily* is offended, and always willing to Compound for *Wrongs*, if not forgive them.

60. He is never Captious, nor Critical; hates *Banter* and *Jests:* He may be Pleasant, but not Light; he never deals but in *Substantial Ware*, and leaves the rest for the *Toy Pates* (or Shops) of the *World*; which are so far from being his Business, that they are not so much as his *Diversion*.

61. He

61. He is always for some solid Good, *Civil* or *Moral*; as, to make his Country more *Vertuous*, Preserve her Peace and Liberty, Imploy her Poor, Improve Land, Advance Trade, Suppress Vice, Incourage Industry, and all Mechanick Knowledge; and that they should be the *Care* of the Government, and the Blessing and Praise of the People.

62. To conclude, He is Just, and *fears God, hates Covetousness, and eschews Evil, and loves his Neighbour as himself.*

Of the Government of Thoughts.

63. Man being made a Reasonable, and so a *Thinking* Creature, there is nothing more *Worthy* of his Being, than the *Right* Direction and Employment of his Thoughts; since upon *This*, depends both his Usefulness to the Publick, and his own present and future Benefit in all Respects.

64. The Consideration of this, has often obliged me to Lament the Unhappiness of Mankind, that through too great a Mixture

and Confusion of Thoughts, have been hardly able to make a Right or Mature Judgment of Things.

65. To this is owing the various *Uncertainty* and *Confusion* we see in the *World*, and the *Intemperate* Zeal that occasions them.

66. To this also is to be attributed the *imperfect* Knowledge we have of Things, and the slow Progress we make in attaining to a Better; like the Children of *Israel* that were *forty* Years upon their Journey, from *Egypt* to *Canaan*, which might have been per-

Reflections and Maxims performed in *Less* than One.

67. In fine, 'tis to this that we ought to ascribe, if not all, at least most of the Infelicities we Labour under.

68. *Clear* therefore thy Head, and *Rally*, and *Manage* thy Thoughts *Rightly*, and thou wilt *Save* Time, and *See* and *Do* thy Business *Well*; for thy Judgment will be *Distinct*, thy Mind *Free*, and the Faculties *Strong* and *Regular*

69. Always remember to *bound* thy Thoughts to the *present* Occasion.

70. If it be thy Religious Duty, suffer nothing else to *Share* in them. And if any Civil or Temporal Affair, observe the same Caution, and thou wilt be a *whole* Man to every Thing, and do *twice* the Business in the same time.

71. If any Point over-Labours thy Mind, divert and relieve it, by some other Subject, of a more *Sensible*, or Manual Nature, rather than what may affect the Understanding; for this were to write one thing
upon

Reflections and Maxims. 29
upon another, which *blots out* our former Impreſſions, or renders them *Illegible.*

72. *They* that are leaſt divided in their Care, always give the beſt Account of their Buſineſs,

73. As therefore thou art always to purſue the *preſent* Subject, till thou haſt maſter'd it, ſo if it fall out that thou haſt more Affairs than one upon thy Hand, be ſure to *prefer* that which is of *moſt* Moment, and will *leaſt* wait thy Leiſure.

74. He

74. He that Judges not well of the Importance of his Affairs, though he may be always *Busy*, he must make but a *small* Progress.

75. But make not more Business necessary than is so; and rather *lessen* than augment *Work* for thy self.

76. Nor yet be *over-eager* in pursuit of any Thing; for the Mercurial too often happen to leave *Judgment* behind them, and sometimes make Work for *Repentance*.

Reflections and Maxims. 31

77. He that *over-runs* his Business, leaves it for him that follows more leasurely to take it up; which has often proved a profitable Harvest to them that never Sow'd.

78. 'Tis the Advantage that flower Tempers have upon the Men of lively Parts, that tho' they don't lead, they will *Follow well, and Glean Clean.*

79. Upon the whole Matter, Employ thy Thoughts as thy Business requires, and let that have Place according to Merit and Urgency; giving every Thing a Review and due Digestion,

stion, and thou wilt prevent many Errors and Vexations, as well as save much time to thy self in the Course of thy Life.

Of Envy.

80. It is the Mark of an ill Nature, to *lessen* good Actions, and *aggravate* ill Ones.

81. Some Men do as much *begrutch* others a good Name, as they want one themselves; and perhaps *that* is the Reason of it.

82. But certainly they are in the Wrong, that can think they are lessened, because others have their *Due*.

83. Such People generally have less Merit than Ambition, that *Covet* the Reward of other Men's; and to be sure a very ill Nature, that will rather *Rob* others of their Due, than allow them their Praise.

84. It is more an Error of our Will, than our Judgment: For we know it to be an Effect of our *Passion*, not our Reason; and therefore we are the more culpable

pable in our *Partial* Estimates.

85. It is as Envious as Unjust, to *under-rate* another's Actions where their intrinsick *Worth* recommends them to disengaged Minds.

86. Nothing shews more the Folly, as well as Fraud of Man, than *Clipping* of Merit and Reputation.

87. And as some Men think it an *Allay* to themselves, that others have their Right; so they know no End of *Pilfering* to raise their own Credit.

88. This

88. This Envy is the Child of *Pride*, and Misgives, rather than Mistakes.

89. It will have Charity, to be *Ostentation*; Sobriety, *Covetousness*; Humility, *Craft*; Bounty, *Popularity*. In short, Vertue must be *Design*, and Religion, only *Interest*. Nay, the best of Qualities must not pass without a **But** to allay their Merit and abate their Praise. *Basest* of Tempers! and they that have them, the *Worst* of Men!

90. But Just and Noble Minds Rejoyce in other Men's Success, and *help* to augment their Praise.

91. And

91. And indeed they are not without a Love to Vertue, that take a Satisfaction in seeing her Rewarded, and such deserve to *share* her Character that do abhor to *lessen* it.

Of Man's Life.

92. Why is Man *less* durable than the Works of his Hands, but because *This is not* the Place of his Rest?

93. And it is a Great and Just Reproach upon him, that he should *fix* his Mind where he cannot *stay* himself.

94. Were

94. Were it not more his *Wisdom* to be concerned about those *Works* that will go with him, and erect a Mansion for him where Time has Power neither over him nor it?

95. 'Tis a sad Thing for *Man* so often to miss his Way to his *Best*, as well as most Lasting Home.

Of Ambition.

96. They that soar too high, often fall *hard*; which makes a *low* and level Dwelling preferable.

97. The

38 Reflections and Maxims.

97. The tallest Trees are most in the Power of the *Winds*, and Ambitious *Men* of the Blasts of Fortune.

98. They are *most* seen and observed, and most envyed: Least Quiet, but most Talk'd of, and not often to their Advantage.

99. Those Builders had need of a good Foundation, that lie so much exposed to *Weather*.

100. Good *Works* are a *Rock*, that will support their Credit; but Ill Ones a Sandy Foundation that

that *Yields* to Calamities.

101. And truly they ought to expect no Pity in their Fall, that when in Power had no *Bowels* for the Unhappy.

102. The worst of Distempers; always Craving and Thirsty, Restless and Hated: A perfect *Delirium* in the Mind: *Insufferable* in Success, and in Disappointments most *Revengeful*.

Of Praise or Applause.

103. We are too apt to love *Praise*, but not to *Deserve* it.

104. But if we would Deserve it, we must love *Virtue* more than That.

105. As their is no Passion in us sooner moved, or more deceiveable, so for that reason there is none over which we ought to be more *Watchful*, whether we give or receive it: For if we give it, we must be sure to mean it, and measure it too.

106. If

Reflections and Maxims. 41

106. If we are *Penurious*, it shows *Emulation*; if we exceed, *Flattery*.

107. *Good Measure* belongs to Good Actions; more looks Nauseous, as well as Insincere; besides, 'tis a *Persecuting* of the Meritorious, who are out of Countenance to *hear*, what they deserve.

108. It is much *easier* for him to *merit* Applause, than *hear* of it: And he never doubts himself more, or the Person that gives it, than when he *hears so much* of it.

109. But

109. But to say true, there needs not *many* Cautions on this Hand, since the *World* is rarely *just enough* to the Deserving.

110. However, we cannot be too Circumspect *how* we receive Praise: For if we Contemplate our selves in a *false* Glass, we are sure to be *mistaken* about our Dues; and because we are too apt to believe what is Pleasing, rather than what is True, we may be too easily swell'd, beyond our just Proportion, by the *Windy* Complements of Men.

111. Make

Reflections and Maxims. 43

111. Make ever therefore *Allowances* for what is said on such Occasions, or thou Exposest, as well as Deceivest thy self.

112. For an over-value of our selves, gives us but a dangerous Security in many Respects.

113. We expect more than belongs to us; take all that's given us tho' never meant us; and fall out with those that are not as *full of us* as we are of our selves.

114. In short, 'tis a Passion that abuses our Judgment,

ment, and makes us both Unsafe and Ridiculous.

115. Be not *fond* therefore of Praise, but *seek* Vertue that leads to it.

116. And yet no more *lessen* or *dissemble* thy Merit, than over-rate it: For tho' Humility be a Vertue, an affected one is none.

Of Conduct in Speech.

117. Enquire *often*, but Judge *rarely*, and thou wilt not often be mistaken.

118 It is safer to Learn, than teach; and who conceals

Reflections and Maxims. 45
ceals his Opinion, has *nothing* to Answer for.

119. Vanity or Resentment often engage us, and 'tis too to one but we come off Losers; for one shews a Want of *Judgment* and *Humility*, as the other does of *Temper* and *Discretion*.

120. Not that I admire the *Reserved*; for they are next to *Unnatural* that are not Communicable. But if Reservedness be at any time a Vertue, 'tis in *Throngs* or *ill* Company.

121. Beware also of *Affectation in Speech*; it often
C 2   wrongs

wrongs *Matter*, and ever shows a *blind* Side.

122. Speak properly, and in as few Words as you can, but always *plainly*; for the End of Speech is not Ostentation but to be understood.

123. They that affect Words more than Matter, will *dry* up that little they have.

124. *Sense* never fails to give them that have it, *Words* enough to make them understood.

125. But

125. But it too often happens in some Conversations, as in *Apothecary-Shops*, that those Pots that are *Empty*, or have Things of small Value in them, are as *gaudily Dress'd* and *Flourish'd*, as those that are full of precious Drugs.

126. This Labouring of slight Matter with flourish'd Turns of Expression, is fulsome, and worse than the *Modern Imitation* of Tapestry, and *East-India* Goods, in Stuffs and Linnens. In short, 'tis but *Tawdry* Talk, and next to very Trash.

Union of Friends.

127. They that love *beyond* the *World*, cannot be seperated by it.

128. Death cannot kill, what *never* dies.

129. Nor can Spirits ever be divided that love and live in the *same* Divine Principle; the *Root* and *Record* of their Friendship.

130. If Absence be not Death, neither is theirs.

131. Death is but *Crossing* the *World*, as Friends do the Seas,

Seas; They live in one another still.

132. For they must needs be present that love and live in that which is *Omnipresent*.

133. In this Divine Glass, they see Face to Face; and their Converse is *Free*, as well as *Pure*.

134. This is the Comfort of Friends, that tho' they may be said to *Die*, yet their Friendship and Society are, in the best Sense, ever present, because *Immortal*.

Of being Easy in Living.

135. 'Tis a Happiness to be delivered from a *Curious* Mind, as well as from a Dainty Palate.

136. For it is not only a Troublesome but *Slavish* Thing to be *Nice*.

137. They *narrow* their own Freedom and Comforts, that make *so much* requisite to enjoy them.

138. To be *Easy* in Living, is much of the *Pleasure* of Life: But difficult Tempers will always want it.

139. A

139. A *Careless* and *Homely* Breeding is therefore preferable to one Nice and Delicate.

140. And he that is taught to live upon a *little*, owes more to his Father's *Wisdom*, than he that has a great deal left him, does to his Father's Care.

141. Children can't well be too hardly Bred: For besides that it *fits* them to bear the *Roughest* Providences, it is more *Masculine*, Active and Healthy.

142. Nay, 'tis certain, that the *Liberty* of the Mind is mightily preserved by it.

For so 'tis served, instead of being a Servant, indeed a Slave to sensual Delicacies.

143. As Nature is soon answered, so are such *satisfied*.

144. The Memory of the Ancients is hardly in any thing more to be celebrated, than in a *Strict and Useful Institution of Youth*.

145. By *Labour* they prevented *Luxury* in their *young* People, till *Wisdom* and Philosophy had taught them to *Resist* and *Despise* it.

146. It must be therefore a gross Fault to strive so hard for the Pleasure of our Bodies, and be so insensible and careless of the *Freedom* of our Souls.

Of Man's Inconsiderateness and Partiality.

147. 'Tis very observable, if our Civil Rights are invaded or incroach'd upon, we are mightily *touch'd*, and *fill* every Place with our Resentment and Complaint, while we suffer our selves, our *Better* and Nobler Selves, to be the *Property* and Vassals of Sin, the *worst* of Invaders.

148. In

148. *In vain* do we expect to be delivered from such Troubles, till we are delivered from the *Cause* of them, our Disobedience to God.

149. When he has his *Dues* from us, it will be *time enough* for Him to give us ours out of one another.

150. 'Tis our great Happiness, if we could understand it, that we meet with such *Checks* in the *Cares* of our worldly Enjoyments, lest we should *Forget* the Giver, adore the Gift, and *terminate* our *Felicity* here, which

which is not Man's *ultimate* Bless.

151. Our Losses are often made *Judgments* by our *Guilt*, and *Mercies* by our *Repentance*.

152. Besides, it argues great Folly in Men to let their Satisfaction exceed the *true Value* of any Temporal Matter: For Disappointments are not always to be measured by the Loss of the Thing, but the *over-value* we put upon it.

153. And thus Men improve their own Miseries, for want of an Equal and Just

Just Estimate of what they Enjoy or Lose.

154. There lies a *Proviso* upon every Thing in this World, and we must observe it at our own Peril, *viz. To love God above all*, and Act for *Judgment*, the *Last* I mean.

Of the Rule of Judging.

155. In all Things *Reason* should prevail: 'Tis quite another Thing to be *stiff* than steady in an Opinion.

156. This may be Reasonable, but that is ever *Wilful*.

157. In such Cases it always happens, that the clearer the Argument, the *greater* the Obstinacy, where the *Design* is not to be convinced.

158. This is to value Humour more than Truth, and prefer a *sullen Pride* to a reasonable Submission.

159. 'Tis the Glory of a Man to *vail* to Truth; as it is the Mark of a good Nature to be *Easily* entreated.

160. Beasts

160. Beasts Act by Sense, Man should by *Reason*; else he is a greater Beast than ever God made: And the Proverb is verified, The Corruption of the best Things is the worst and most offensive.

161. A reasonable Opinion must ever be in Danger, where Reason is not Judge.

162. Tho' there is a Regard due to Education, and the Tradition of our Fathers, Truth will ever *deserve* as well as claim the Preference.

163. If like *Theophilus* and *Timothy*, we have been brought up in the Knowledge of the best Things, 'tis our Advantage: But neither they nor we *lose* by trying their Truth; for so we learn their, as well as it's *intrinsick Worth*.

164. Truth never lost Ground by Enquiry, because she is *most of all Reasonable*.

165. Nor can that need another Authority, that is *Self-evident*.

166. If my own Reason be *on the Side* of a Principle,

with what can I Dispute or withstand it?

167. And if Men would once consider one another reasonably, they would either reconcile their Differences, or *more Amicably* maintain them.

168. Let That therefore be the Standard, that has *most to say* for it self; Tho' of that let *every Man* be Judge for himself.

169. Reason, like the *Sun*, is *Common* to All; And 'tis for want of examining all *by* the *same* Light and Measure, that we are not all of the *same* Mind.
For

For all have it to that End, though all do not use it *So*.

Of Formality.

170. Form is Good, but not *Formality*.

171. In the Use of the best of Forms there is too much of that I fear.

172. 'Tis absolutely necessary, that this Distinction should go along with People in their Devotion; for too many are apter to rest upon *What* they do, than *How* they do their Duty.

173. If it were considered, that it is the *Frame* of the Mind that gives our Performances Acceptance, *we* would lay more Stress on our *Inward* Preparation than our Outward Action.

Of the mean Notion we have of God.

174. Nothing more shews the low Condition Man is fallen into, than the *unsuitable* Notion we must have of God, by the *Ways* we take to please him.

175. As if it availed any thing to him that we performed so many Ceremonies

nies and external Forms of Devotion, who never meant more by them, than to try our Obedience, and, through them, to shew us something *more Excellent and Durable* beyond them.

176. Doing, while we are *Undoing,* is good for nothing.

177. Of what Benefit is it to say our *Prayers* regularly, go to *Church*, receive the *Sacraments*, and may be go to *Confessions* too; ay, *Feast* the Priest, and give *Alms* to the Poor, and yet *Lye, Swear, Curse,* be *Drunk, Covetous, Unclean, Proud, Revengeful,*

Revengeful, *Vain* and *Idle* at the same time?

178. Can one excuse or ballance the other? Or will God think himself well served, where his Law is *Violated*? Or well used, where there is so much more *Shew* than Substance?

179. 'Tis a most dangerous Error for a Man to think to excuse himself in the Breach of a Moral Duty, by a *Formal* Performance of *Positive Worship*; and less when of Human Invention.

Reflections and Maxims. 65

180. Our Blessed Saviour most rightly and clearly distinguished and determined this Case, when he told the *Jews*, that they were his *Mother*, his *Brethren* and *Sisters*, who did the *Will* of his Father.

Of the Benefit of Justice.

181. Justice is a great Support of Society, because an *Insurance* to all Men of their Property: This violated, there's no Security, which throws all into *Confusion* to recover it.

182. An Honest Man is a fast *Pledge* in Dealing. A Man is *Sure* to have

have it if it be *to be had*.

183. Many are so, meerly of *Necessity*. Others not so only for the same Reason: But such an honest Man is *not* to be thanked, and such a dishonest Man is to be *pity'd*.

184. But he that is dishonest for Gain, is *next* to a Robber, and to be punish'd for Example.

185. And indeed there are *few* Dealers, but what are Faulty, which makes Trade *Difficult*, and a great *Temptation* to Men of *Vertue*.

186. 'Tis

186. 'Tis not what they should, but what they *can* get: Faults or Decays must be concealed: Big Words given, where they are not deserved, and the Ignorance or Necessity of the Buyer imposed upon for unjust Profit.

187. These are the Men that keep their Words for their own Ends, and are only Just for Fear of the Magistrate.

188. A *Politick* rather than a Moral Honesty; a *constrained*, not a chosen Justice: According to the Proverb, *Patience per Force,*
and

and *thank you for nothing.*

189. But of all Justice, that is the greatest, that passes under the Name of Law. A Cut-Purse in *Westminster-Hall* exceeds; for that advances Injustice to Oppression, where Law is alledged for that which it should punish.

Of Jealousy.

190. The Jealous are Troublesome to others, but a *Torment* to themselves.

191. Jea-

191. Jealousy is a kind of *Civil War* in the Soul, where *Judgment* and *Imagination* are at perpetual *Jars*.

192. This Civil *Dissention* in the Mind, like that of the Body Politick, commits great Disorders, and lays all waste.

193. Nothing stands safe in it's *Way*: *Nature, Interest, Religion,* must Yield to it's Fury.

194. It Violates *Contracts*, Dissolves *Society*, Breaks *Wedlock*, Betrays *Friends* and *Neighbours*. *No Body* is Good, and every one

is either doing or designing them a *Mischief*.

195. It has a *Venome* that more or less rankles where-ever it Bites: And as it reports Fancies for Facts, so it *disturbs* it's *own* House as often as other Folks.

196. It's Rise is *Guilt* or *Ill Nature*, and by Reflection thinks it's own Faults to be other Men's; as he that's over-run with the *Jaundice* takes others to be *Yellow*.

197. A Jealous Man only sees his *own Spectrum*, when he looks upon other Men,

Men, and gives his Character in theirs.

Of State.

198. I love Service, but not *State*; One is Useful, the Other *Superfluous*.

199. The *Trouble* of this, as well as Charge, is Real; but the Advantage only Imaginary.

200. Besides, it helps to set us up *above our selves*, and Augments our Temptation to Disorder.

201. The *Least* Thing out of Joynt, or omitted, makes us uneasy, and we are ready to think our selves ill served, about that which is of no real Service at all. Or so much better than other Men, as we have the Means of greater State.

202. But this is all for want of *Wisdom*, which carries the *truest* and most forceable *State* along with it.

203. He that makes not himself *Cheap* by indiscreet Conversation, puts Value enough upon himself every where.

204. The

204. The other is rather Pageantry than State.

Of a Good Servant.

205. A True, and a Good Servant, are the same Thing.

206. But no *Servant* is True to his Master, that Defrauds him.

207. Now there are many Ways of Defrauding a Master, as, of *Time, Care, Pains, Respect* and *Reputation*, as well as *Money*.

208. He

208. He that Neglects his Work, Robs his Master, since he is Fed and Paid as if he did his Best; and he that is not as Diligent in the Absence, as in the Presence of his Master, cannot be a true Servant.

209. Nor is he a true Servant, that buys dear to *share* in the Profit with the Seller.

210. Nor yet he that tells Tales without Doors; or deals basely in his Master's Name with other People; or Connives at others Loyterings, Wasteings,

Reflections and Maxims 75
ings, or dishonourable Reflections.

211. So that a true *Servant* is *Diligent, Secret* and *Respectful*: More *Tender* of his Master's Honour and Interest, than of his own Profit.

212. Such a *Servant* deserves well, and if Modest under his Merit, should liberally feel it at his Master's Hand.

Of an Immediate Pursuit of the World.

213. It shews a *Depraved* State of Mind, to *Cark*

and

and Care for that which one does not need.

214. Some are as eager to be *Rich*, as ever they were to Live: For *Superfluity*, as for Subsistance.

215. But that *Plenty* should augment *Coveteousness*, is a *Perversion* of Providence; and yet the Generality are the *worse* for their Riches.

216. But it is strange, that *Old* Men should excel For generally Money lies nearest them that are nearest their *Graves*: As if they would augment their Love in Proportion to the *little Time*

Time they have left to enjoy it: And yet their Pleasure is without Enjoyment, since none enjoy what they do *not use*.

217. So that instead of learning to leave their great Wealth easily, they hold the *Faster*, because they must leave it: So *Sordid* is the Temper of some Men.

218. Where *Charity* keeps Pace with Gain, Industry is blessed: But to slave to get, and keep it *Sordidly*, is a *Sin* against *Providence*, a Vice in *Government*, and an Injury to their *Neighbours*.

219. Such

219. Such are they as spend not one *Fifth* of their Income, and, it may be, give not one *Tenth* of what they spend to the Needy.

220. This is the *worst* sort of Idolatry, because there can be *no Religion* in it, nor Ignorance pleaded in *Excuse* of it; and that it wrongs other Folks that ought to have a *Share* therein.

Of the Interest of the Publick in our Estates.

221. *Hardly* any Thing is given us for our *Selves*, but the Publick may claim

Reflections and Maxims. 79
a *Share* with us. But of all we call ours, we are *most accountable* to God and the Publick for our Estates: In this we are but *Stewards*, and to *Hord* up all to our selves is great *Injustice* as well as Ingratitude.

222. If all Men were so far *Tenants* to the Publick, that the *Superfluities* of Gain and Expence were applyed to the *Exigencies* thereof, it would put an *End* to Taxes, leave never a Beggar, and make the greatest *Bank* for National Trade in *Europe*.

223. It is a *Judgment* upon us, as well as *Weakness*, tho' we

we wont see it, to begin at the *wrong* End.

224. If the Taxes we give are not to maintain Pride, I am sure there would be less, if *Pride* were made a *Tax* to the Government.

225. I confess I have wondered that so many Lawful and Useful Things are Excised by Laws, and *Pride* left to *Reign Free* over them and the Publick.

226. But since People are more afraid of the *Laws* of Man than of God, because their Punishment seems to be

Reflections and Maxims.

be *nearest:* I know not how Magistrates can be excused in their suffering such *Excess* with *Impunity.*

227. Our Noble *English Patriarchs* as well as *Patriots*, were so sensible of this Evil, that they made several excellent Laws, commonly called *Sumptuary*, to *Forbid*, at least *Limit* the *Pride* of the People; which because the Execution of them would be our Interest and Honour, their Neglect must be our just Reproach and Loss.

228. 'Tis but Reasonable that the Punishment of *Pride* and Excess should help to

to *support* the Government, since it must otherwise inevitably be ruined *by them.*

229. But some say, *It ruins Trade,* and will make the *Poor* Burthensome to the Publick: But if such Trade in Consequence ruins the Kingdom, *is it not time to ruin that* Trade? Is Moderation no part of our Duty, and Temperance an *Enemy* to Government?

230. He is a *Judas* that will get Money by any Thing.

Reflections and Maxims. 83

231. To *wink* at a Trade that effeminates the People, and invades the Ancient Discipline of the Kingdom, is a Crime Capital, and to be severely punish'd instead of being *excused* by the *Magistrate*.

232. Is there no *better* Employment for the Poor than *Luxury*? *Miserable Nation!*

233. What did they before they fell into these *forbidden* Methods? Is there not Land enough in *England* to Cultivate, and more and better Manufactures to be Made?

234. Have

84 *Reflections and Maxims.*

234. Have we no room for them in our *Plantations*, about Things that may augment *Trade*, without *Luxury*?

235. In short, let *Pride pay*, and *Excess* be *well Excised* And if that will not *Cure* the People, it will *help to Keep the Kingdom*.

The Vain Man.

236. But a *Vain* Man is a *Nauseous* Creature: He is so *full* of *himself* that he has *no Room* for any thing else, be it never so Good or Deserving.

237. 'Tis

Reflections and Maxims. 85

237. 'Tis *I* at every turn that *does* this, or *can* do that. And as he abounds in his *Comparisons*, so he is sure to give himself the *better* of *every Body* else; according to the Proverb, *All his Geese are Swans.*

238. They are certainly to be pity'd that can be so much *mistaken* at *Home*

239. And yet I have sometimes thought that such People are in a sort Happy, that nothing can put *out of Countenance* with themselves, though they neither have nor merit other Peoples.

240. But

240. But at the same time one would wonder they should not *feel* the Blows they give themselves, or get from others, for this intolerable and ridiculous *Temper*, nor shew any Concern at that which makes others *blush* for, as well as at them *(viz.)* their *unreasonable* Assurance.

241. To be a Man's own Fool is bad enough, but the Vain Man is *Every Body's*.

242. This silly Disposition comes of a Mixture of *Ignorance*, *Confidence* and *Pride*; and as there is more

or less of the last, so it is more or less offensive or Entertaining.

243. And yet perhaps the worst part of this Vanity is it's *Unteachableness*. Tell it any Thing, and it has known it long ago; and out-runs Information and Instruction, or else proudly *puffs* at it.

244. Whereas the greatest Understandings doubt most, are readiest to learn, and least pleas'd with themselves; this, with *no Body else*.

245. For tho' they stand on *higher* Ground, and so see *further* than their Neighbours,

bours, they are yet *humbled* by their Prospect, since it shews them something, *so much higher* and above their Reach.

246. And truly then it is, that Sense shines with the greatest Beauty when it is set in *Humility*.

247. An *humble* able Man is a *Jewel* worth a Kingdom: It is often saved by him, as *Solomon*'s *Poor Wise Man* did the City.

248. May we have more of *them*, or less *Need* of them.

The Conformist.

249. It is reasonable to concur where Conscience does not forbid a Compliance; for Conformity is at least a **Civil Vertue**.

250. But we should only press it in *Necessaries*, the rest may prove a *Snare* and Temptation to *break* Society.

251. But above all, it is a *Weakness* in Religion and Government, where it is carried to things of an Indifferent Nature, since besides that it makes way for Scruples,

Scruples, *Liberty is* always the *Price* of it.

252. Such Conformists have little to *boast* of, and therefore the less Reason to Reproach others that have more Latitude.

253. And yet the *Latitudinarian* that I love, is one that is only so in Charity, for the Freedom I recommend is no *Scepticism* in Judgment, and much less so in Practice.

The

The Obligations of Great Men to Almighty God.

254. It seems but reasonable that those whom God has *Distinguish'd* from others, by his *Goodness*, should distinguish themselves to him by their *Gratitude*.

255. For tho' he has made of *One* Blood all Nations, he has not rang'd or dignified them upon the *Level*, but in a sort of Subordination and Dependency.

92 *Reflections and Maxims.*

256. If we look upwards we find it in the Heavens, where the *Planets* have their several Degrees of Glory, and so the other *Stars* of Magnitude and Lustre.

257. If we look upon the Earth, we see it among the *Trees* of the Wood, from the *Cedar* to the *Bramble*; in the *Waters* among the *Fish*, from the *Leviathan* to the *Sprat*; in the *Air* among the *Birds*, from the *Eagle* to the *Sparrow*; among the *Beasts*, from the *Lyon* to the *Cat*; and among *Mankind* it self, from the *King* to the *Scavenger*.

258. Our

258. Our Great Men, doubtless, were designed by the *Wise* Framer of the World for our *Religious, Moral* and *Politick* Planets; for *Lights* and *Directions* to the lower Ranks of the numerous Company of their own Kind, both in Precepts and Examples; and they are well paid for their Pains too, who have the Honour and Service of their fellow Creatures, and the *Marrow* and *Fat* of the Earth for their Share.

259. But is it not a most unaccountable Folly, that Men should be *Proud* of the Providences that should

Humble them? Or think the *Better* of themselves, instead of *Him* that raised them so much above the Level; or in being so in their Lives, in return of his Extraordinary Favours.

260. But it is but too near *a-kin* to us, to think no farther than *our selves*, either in the *Acquisition*, or *Use* of our Wealth and Greatness; when, alas, they are the *Preferments of Heaven*, to try our *Wisdom*, Bounty and Gratitude.

261. 'Tis a dangerous Perversion of the End of Providence to *Consume* the *Time, Power* and *Wealth*
he

he has given us above other Men, to gratify our *Sordid Passions*, instead of playing the good Stewards, to the Honour of our great Benefactor, and the Good of our fellow-Creatures.

262. But it is an Injustice too, since those Higher Ranks of Men are but the *Trustees* of Heaven for the Benefit of lesser Mortals, who, as *Minors*, are intituled to all their Care and Provision.

263. For tho' God has dignified some Men above their Brethren, it never was to serve their Pleasures, but that

that they might take Pleasure to serve the Publick.

264. For this Cause doubtless it was that they were raised above Necessity or any Trouble to Live, that they might have more Time and Ability to Care for Others: And 'tis certain, where that *Use* is not made of the Bounties of Providence, they are *Imbezzell'd* and Wasted.

265. It has often struck me with a serious Reflection, when I have observed the great Inequality of the World; that *one* Man should have *such Numbers* of his fellow Creatures,

Reflections and Maxims. 97
tures, to *Wait* upon him, who have Souls to be saved as well as he; and this not for Business, but *State.* Certainly a poor Employment of his Money, and a worse of their Time.

266. But that any one Man should make work for so many; or rather keep them from *Work*, to make up a *Train*, has a *Levity* and *Luxury* in it very reprovable, both in Religion and Government.

267. But even in allowable Services it has an humbling Consideration, and what should raise the
Thank-

Thankfulness of the Great Men to him that has so much better'd their Circumstances, and *Moderated* the Use of their Dominion over those of their own Kind.

268. When the poor *Indians* hear us call any of our Family by the Name of *Servants*, they cry out, *What, call Brethren Servants!* We call our *Dogs* Servants, but never *Men*. The *Moral* certainly can do us no Harm, but may Instruct us, to *abate* our Hight, and *narrow* our *State* and Attendance.

269. And

Reflections and Maxims. 99

269. And what has been said of their Excess, may in some measure be apply'd to other Branches of Luxury, that set *ill Examples* to the lesser World, and R.. the Needy of their Pensions.

270. GOD Almighty *Touch* the Hearts of our *Grandees* with a Sense of his *Distinguish'd* Goodness, and that true End of it, that they may better distinguish themselves in their Conduct, to the Glory of Him that has thus liberally Preferr'd them, and the Benefit of their fellow Creatures.

Of Refining upon other Men's Actions or Interests.

271. This seems to be the *Master-Piece* of our Politicians: But no Body shoots more at *Random*, than those Refiners.

272. A perfect *Lottery*, and meer *Hap-hazard*. Since the true Spring of the Actions of Men is as *Invisible* as their Hearts; and so are their *Thoughts* too of their several Interests.

273. He that judges of other Men by himself, does not always hit the Mark, because all Men have not the

the same Capacity, nor *Passions* in Interest.

274. If an *able* Man refines upon the Proceedings of an *ordinary* Capacity, according to his own, he must ever miss it: But much more the ordinary Man when he shall pretend to speculate the *Motives* to the Able Man's Actions: For the Able Man, deceives himself by making t'other wiser than he is in the Reason of his Conduct; and the ordinary Man makes himself so, in presuming to judge of the Reasons of the Abler Man's Actions.

275. 'Tis

275. 'Tis in short, a *Wood*, a *Maze*; and of nothing are we more *uncertain*, nor in any thing do we oftner *befool* our selves.

276. The Mischiefs are many that follow this Humour, and dangerous: For Men *Misguide* themselves, act upon *false Measures*, and meet frequently with *mischievous Disappointments*.

277. It excludes all *Confidence* in Commerce; allows of no such Thing as a *Principle* in Practice; supposes every Man to act upon other Reasons than what appears, and that there is no such thing as a *Staightness*

ness or *Sincerity* among Mankind: A Trick instead of Truth.

278. Neither, allowing Nature or Religion; but some worldly Fetch or Advantage: The true, the hidden Motive to all Men to act or do.

279. 'Tis hard to express it's *Uncharitableness*, as well as *Uncertainty*; and has more of *Vanity* than Benefit in it.

280. This Foolish Quality gives a large Field, but let what I have said serve for this Time.

Of Charity.

281. Charity has various Senses, but is *Excellent* in all of them.

282. It imports; first, the *Commiseration* of the Poor, and Unhappy of Mankind, and extends an *Helping-Hand* to mend their Condition.

283. They that feel nothing of this, are at best not above *half* of Kin to Humane Race; since they must have *no Bowels*, which makes such an *Essential* Part thereof, who have no more Nature.

284. A

284. A Man, and yet not have the Feeling of the *Wants* or *Needs* of his own Flesh and Blood! A *Monster* rather! And may he never be suffer'd to propagate such an unnatural Stock in the World.

285. Such an Uncharitableness *spoils* the best Gains, and two to one but it entails a Curse upon the Possessors.

286. Nor can we expect to be heard of God in our *Prayers*, that turn the *deaf Ear* to the Petitions of the Distressed amongst our fellow Creatures.

287. God

287. God sends the Poor to *try* us, as well as he tries them by being such: And he that refuses them a little out of the great deal that God has given him, *Lays up Poverty* in Store for his own Posterity.

288. I will not say these Works are *Meritorious*, but dare say they are *Acceptable*, and go not without their Reward. Tho' to Humble us in our Fulness and Liberality too, we only Give but what is given us to *Give* as well as use; for if we are *not our own*, less is *that so* which God has intrusted us with.

289. Next,

289. Next, CHARITY makes the *best* Construction of *Things* and *Persons*, and is so far from being an evil Spy, a Back biter, or a Detractor, that it *excuses Weakness, extenuates* Miscarriages, makes the *best* of every Thing; forgives *every Body*, serves *All*, and hopes to the End.

290. It *moderates* Extreams, is always for *Expediences*, *labours* to *accommodate* Differences, and had rather *Suffer* than Revenge: And so far from Exacting the *utmost Farthing*, that it had rather *lose* than seek her Own *Violently*.

291. As

291. As it acts Freely, so, Zealously too; but 'tis always to *do Good*, for it hurts *no Body*.

292. An *Universal Remedy* against Discord, and an Holy Cement for Mankind.

293. And *lastly*, 'Tis *Love to God and the Brethren*, which raises the Soul *above* all worldly Considerations; and, as it gives a *Taste* of Heaven *upon* Earth, so 'tis *Heaven* in the Fulness of it hereafter to the truly Charitable here.

294. This

294. This is the *Noblest* Sense Charity has, after which all should press, as that more Excellent *Way*.

295. Nay, *most* Excellent, for as *Faith*, *Hope* and *Charity* were the more Excellent *Way* that Great Apostle discovered to the Christians (too apt to stick in *Outward Gifts* and *Church Performances*) so of that better *Way* he preferr'd *Charity* as the *best* Part, because it would *out-last* the rest, and abide for ever.

296. Wherefore a Man can never be a true and good Christian without Charity, even in the lowest Sense of it;

it: And yet he may have that Part thereof, and still be none of the Apostle's *true Christian*, since he tells us, That tho' we should give all our Goods to the Poor, and *want Charity* (in her other and higher Senses) *it would profit us nothing*.

297. Nay, tho' we had *All Tongues*, *All Knowleage*, and even *Gifts* of *Prophesy*, and were *Preachers* to others; ay, and had Zeal enough to *give* our *Bodies to be burned*, yet if we *wanted Charity* it would not avail us for Salvation.

298. It

298. It seems it was his (and indeed ought to be our) *Unum Necessarium*, or the One Thing Needful, which our Saviour attributed to *Mary* in *Preferrence* to her Sister *Martha*, that seems not to have wanted the lesser Parts of Charity.

299. Would God this Divine Vertue were more *implanted* and *diffused* among Mankind, the *Pretenders* to *Christianity* especially, and we should certainly mind *Piety more than Controversy*, and *Exercise Love and Compassion instead of Censuring and Persecuting one another in any manner whatsoever*.

FINIS.

THE INDEX.

The Right Moralist   Page 1.
The World's Able Man   p 7.
The Wise Man   p. 20.
Of the Government of Thoughts   p. 25.
Of Envy   p. 32.
Of Man's Life   p. 36.
Of Ambition   p. 37.
Of Praise or Applause   p. 40.
Of Conduct in Speech   p. 44.
Union of Friends   p. 48.
Of being Easy in Living   p. 50.
Of Man's Inconsiderateness and Partiality   p. 53.
Of the Rule of Judging   p. 56.

The INDEX.

Of Formality　　　　　　p. 61.
Of the mean Notion we have
　of God　　　　　　　　p. 62.
Of the Benefit of Justice　p. 65.
Of Jealousy　　　　　　　p. 68.
Of State　　　　　　　　p. 71.
Of a good Servant　　　　p. 73.
Of an Immoderate Pursuit of
　the World　　　　　　　p. 75.
Of the Interest of the Publick
　in our Estates　　　　　p. 78.
The Vain Man　　　　　　p. 84.
The Conformist　　　　　p. 89.
The Obligations of Great Men
　to Almighty God　　　　p. 91.
Of Refining upon other Men's
　Actions or Interests　p. 100.
Of Charity　　　　　　　p. 104.